2, 5 AND 10 TIMES TABLES

CONTENTS

INTRODUCTION	1
WORKING WITH 2S	4
WORKING WITH 5S	16
WORKING WITH 10S	24

About this book

The activities in this book are intended to help children at Key Stage 1/Primary 1–3 understand the multiplication patterns and number facts in the 2, 5 and 10 times tables. Many of these activities are suitable for Reception/P1 children; but most of them are more appropriate to pupils in Year 2/P3, given the relative difficulty of multiplication (and, in England, the progression within the National Numeracy Strategy *Framework for Teaching Mathematics*).

The main resource used in these activities is the A1 poster provided with this book. Some of the suggested activities do not require the poster; but whatever the children are doing, it would be helpful to keep it on display in the classroom. Some of the activities involve using the photocopiable sheets provided at the end of each section. These resource sheets are versatile, and can be adapted for more general use in other mathematics lessons (especially if you are working within the National Numeracy Strategy framework).

This book aims to reinforce individual multiplication facts in the context of mental and oral work and revision activities, and to demonstrate how you can use visual materials to help children understand number facts. Each lesson plan suggests what resources are needed and how the class might be organized. Where appropriate, ideas for assessment, differentiation and extension are suggested. More generally, differentiation will be by outcome, or will be achieved through your choice of questions to ask different children.

INTRODUCTION

About times tables

A grid indicating this book's coverage of statements in all the UK curriculum documents is given on the inside back cover.

It is expected that by the age of 11, all children should know the multiplication facts up to 10 × 10 and have a range of strategies for calculating those facts that they cannot recall. Fundamental number skills such as an understanding of place value and number patterns are also crucial to the children's mathematical work.

In England, the National Numeracy Strategy offers a framework for the teaching of number. Alongside the National Curriculum Programmes of Study, this provides a clear set of guidelines about what is required for all children. The structure of individual lessons is outlined as usually involving whole-class work, frequent and regular mental and oral sessions, and plenary discussions – all at a brisk pace. The activities suggested here are designed to be suitable for this framework.

Links with division

Some of these activities are closely related to division activities. For example, joining dots in multiples of 5 could easily become *How many groups of dots before you get to 35?* It is obviously desirable to make links where appropriate. However, the primary purpose of each activity is to emphasize the skills and language of multiplication. Take care not to gloss over the introduction of aspects of division that would be better addressed through specific activities. If any of the pupils refer to 'sharing', it is probably safe to develop this further; but do not over-emphasize the link at this stage.

About the poster

On the full-colour side of the A1 poster provided with this book, there are clear representations of the 2 and 5 times tables. Beside each number sentence is a pictorial representation of that number fact on a pegboard. This helps the children to relate the abstract number facts to a commonplace classroom resource. It is important for their understanding that they develop a feel for the size and pattern of number facts; this is often achieved through using practical resources.

Some of the suggested activities in this book require such resources. A pegboard gives children the opportunity to count and then organize pegs in order to show a real example of a number. This can also help with their understanding of place value; for example, children can see more clearly that 20 is a greater number than 10 when they have to count out pegs instead of writing down a 2 and a 0. The use of colour is intended to illustrate the repeating patterns of number facts, helping the children to calculate number facts beyond those shown in the poster.

The black and white side of the poster shows a similar pictorial representation of the 10 times table, including the pegboards. As with the full-colour side, this could be used to stimulate the children to make the patterns using real pegboards. Two number grids are also shown:

◆ **1–16 square grid.** Number squares such as this provide opportunities to investigate patterns and relationships between numbers. For example, after using photocopiable page 27, the children could be asked to tell you what they notice about the star patterns within the 1–16 square.

◆ **1–25 square grid.** The patterns in this number square relate to the 5 times table; the children can use it to consider multiples of 5, differences between numbers and other patterns. Some of the activities are based on the use of this grid.

Preparing to use the poster

The poster is designed to be used and seen by the whole class. It is more than a wall display, however: it ought to be an integral part of your teaching. It could be laminated, used with a board or flip chart, or placed on a table-top for group work or games.

However the poster is used, 'Post-it' notes and a board or flip chart should also be available so that the children's ideas can be recorded. Small pieces of card

INTRODUCTION

and Blu-Tack can be used to hide numbers on the poster. Photocopies of the number grids could be laminated for separate use.

You can use the poster as a resource outside specific maths sessions by displaying it on the wall and posing ongoing challenges (verbally or on daily or weekly 'challenge cards') about the number patterns shown – for example: *Can you find a number that is in both the 2 and 5 times tables?* or *Find me an answer from the 5 times tables that is bigger than 20 and even.* It is good practice to ask questions that have more than one possible 'correct' answer. Also (as OFSTED advise), it is best not simply to accept the first 'correct' answer given, but to explore the methods and strategies the children have used to arrive at their answers – including inaccurate ones.

Useful resources

The following resources will be useful for the activities in this book: coloured pegs and pegboards; 1–6 and 0–9 dice; number lines; dominoes, Multilink cubes and individual number cards; pegs and a length of string (to make a 'washing line' for numbers).

Pegboards and coloured pegs like those shown on the poster are available from suppliers such as NES Arnold and county suppliers; so are items such as number lines, 1–6 dice and 0–9 dice. A particularly useful resource in the context of the National Numeracy Strategy is a 'washing line' for numbers; an example is available from the Hamilton Project, Hamilton Education Ltd, Temple Court, 107 Oxford Road, Oxford OX4 2ER (tel. 01865 396613).

LET'S LOOK AT THE POSTER

GROUP SIZE AND ORGANIZATION
Whole class.
DURATION
20–30 minutes.
LEARNING OBJECTIVE
To become familiar with the 'times tables' poster. To appreciate the number patterns and pegboard pictures shown.

YOU WILL NEED
The A1 colour poster; some pegboards and pegs.

WHAT TO DO
This activity is designed to introduce the theme by drawing attention to the pictures and number patterns on the poster. The language used will need to be matched to the age of the children. For example, avoid the term 'multiple' unless you feel the children are ready for it.

Display the colour poster in a prominent position at child-eye level, and gather the children around. Ask them to describe what they can see on the poster:

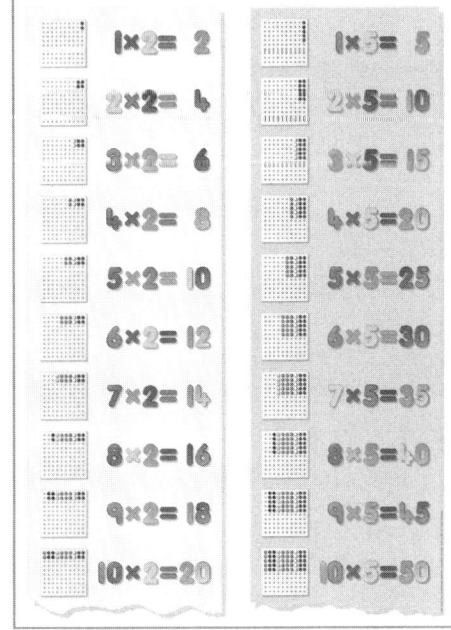

◆ What numbers do you think it is showing?
◆ Can you describe the patterns in any way?
◆ Can you describe these patterns using numbers? (For example, 'Going up in 2s.')
◆ Can you describe the patterns without using numbers? (For example, 'The rows are all the same length.')
◆ Are there any numbers that are in both the 2 and the 5 times tables?
◆ Can you describe the sequence (or pattern) of numbers for each table?
◆ Can you find the numbers in the 5 times table that are not in the 2 times table? Choose some large multiples of 5 and ask whether these are in the 2 times table (for example, 50 or 75).
◆ How do we know whether a number is in the 2 times table? Using a real pegboard, demonstrate how to place a multiple of 2. (Be careful to follow the exact arrangement shown on the poster: 10 × 2 and 2 × 10 are shown differently.)
◆ Point to an example of a 'pair of multiplications', such as 2 × 5 = 10 and 5 × 2 = 10. *Can you see any other pairs?*

Recap on any significant answers. Make the poster an important feature of the classroom, as you might do with a number line.

WORKING WITH 2S

COUNT THEM OUT

GROUP SIZE AND ORGANIZATION
Whole class in suitable space (see below).
DURATION
20 minutes.
LEARNING OBJECTIVE
To be able to count objects in 2s to at least 20.

Figure 1

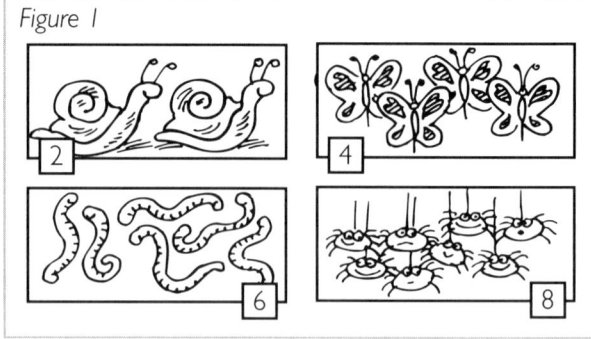

YOU WILL NEED
A number line, the colour poster.

WHAT TO DO
This activity could be done on the carpet, but you will need space for ten children to stand (perhaps in a line at the front) so that the others can see them.

Explain that we have lots of visible body parts 'in 2s'. Ask the children to give you examples. Someone may suggest 'arms' or 'eyes'. Ask: *What items of clothing come in 2s?* (Shoes, gloves and so on.)

Ask for ten volunteers to come and stand at the front; then ask them to put their arms behind their backs, so the class can't see them.
◆ *How many arms can we see?* (Establish '0' as the answer.)
Now ask your volunteers, one at a time, to put out their arms and keep them held out. Each time a 'new' child puts out his or her arms, ask the rest of the class how many arms they can see. Link the number of children with the number of arms: *One child has two arms, two children have four arms...*

Now ask the children to put down their arms (one child at a time). Repeat the questions.

Next, repeat the process; but ask the children to look at the numbers on the number line as well as saying the numbers. It will help if you ask someone to be the 'pointer' on the number line. The ten volunteers may now sit down!

Now ask the children to look at the colour poster. Point to the sets of dots representing the 2s. Ask for a volunteer to come and find one set of 2, then two sets of 2 (showing 4), then sets showing 6 and so on through to 20 – each time, relating the number to the number line.
◆ *How high can we count in 2s?*
◆ *Can we find these numbers on our class number line?*

ASSESSMENT
You could assess a few children by using the two-dot pattern on the poster: ask them to point to each dot pattern and to say the number of dots (counting on in 2s to 20).

IDEAS FOR DISPLAY
Arrangements of pictures similar in format to the dot patterns could be displayed, with the corresponding number written on a card underneath each picture (as in Figure 1). At some stage, you could remove some of the cards and challenge the children to tell you which numbers are missing and where they should go.

WORKING WITH 2S

IDEAS FOR DIFFERENTIATION
To reinforce the concept of counting in 2s, repeat the 'object counting' in different contexts: shoes, ears and so on.

To make the activity more challenging, demonstrate counting in 2s, but miss out a number (with a slight pause) – for example, '2, 4, – 8, 10'. Can the children identify the missing number? They could practise doing this with their partners, going up to whatever number they can. A further challenge might be to ask whether anyone can count backwards, in 2s, from 20.

JOIN THE DOTS

GROUP SIZE AND ORGANIZATION
This activity can be done in pairs, but lends itself more to individual work.
DURATION
10–15 minutes.
LEARNING OBJECTIVE
To count on in 2s. To recognize even numbers.

YOU WILL NEED
Photocopiable page 11, pencils.

WHAT TO DO
Talk with the children about how dot-to-dot puzzles work. Give each child a copy of photocopiable page 11 and a pencil. Explain that they need to start on the number 2 and count on in 2s, joining up the dots. Say that these numbers are called **even** numbers, and that they are **multiples** of 2.

ASSESSMENT
If the child joins the numbers in the correct sequence, a recognizable picture of a duck should appear.

IDEAS FOR DISPLAY
Some children can design their own dot-to-dot puzzles involving other sequences of numbers (see below). A large-scale display of dot-to-dot puzzles can be put on the wall and other children invited to guess what the hidden pictures are.

IDEAS FOR DIFFERENTIATION
This activity is not as easy as it looks. To complete the picture, the children need to be able to recognize and count in multiples of 2. More able children could go on to design their own puzzles using multiples of 5 or 10. Invite them to describe the methods they used.

EQUAL TOWERS

GROUP SIZE AND ORGANIZATION
Whole class, then table groups.
DURATION
40–50 minutes.
LEARNING OBJECTIVE
To identify even numbers.

YOU WILL NEED
Interlocking cubes (enough for every child to have 20), a flip chart and marker pen (or chalkboard and chalk), the poster (both sides).

WHAT TO DO
Ask each child to pick up ten cubes. Now ask them to put the cubes into two equal towers. *Is it possible?* You may need to discuss with them what you mean by 'equal'.

Ask the children to explain what has happened. Now ask them to try with eight cubes. *What happens?*

Now ask them to try with 11 cubes. *What happens? Why?* (The towers cannot be made 'equal', because there is one cube too many.)

Now write some numbers on the flip chart for them to try, or give different groups different sets of numbers. Suggest numbers such as 8, 7, 5, 12, 3, 4, 9, 16, 20 and 19. The children do not all have to try all the numbers; but between the whole class, they should all be attempted.

After 10–15 minutes, ask the children to stop. Talk about what they have found out. Look at the 1–16 number grid on the black and white poster; cover those numbers which the children have identified as 'not working'. Now talk about the numbers still showing: these numbers can be made into two equal towers, and are called 'even' numbers.

WORKING WITH 2S

Encourage the children to tell you which numbers are even, using sentences such as '6 is an even number.' Refer to the two-dot patterns on the colour poster: these numbers each make two equal towers. *Can we say the even numbers, starting with 2? How far can we go? Who can carry on? Will 30 be in the list? How do you know? What about 31? 35? 50?*

Encourage the children to focus on the last digit of an even number by writing them in columns, in order, on the flip chart or board:

2	4	6	8	10
12	14	16	18	20
22	24	...		

◆ *What do you notice?*
◆ *Do you notice the '2, 4, 6, 8, 0' pattern?*

ASSESSMENT
Note whether the children can use interlocking cubes to find out whether a given number is even. Can they identify all the even numbers to 20?

IDEAS FOR DISPLAY
Display a number grid (a photocopy of one of the grids from the black and white poster, or a 0–99 grid) with the odd numbers covered up. Add a label stating: *The numbers we can see are even numbers*. Later, cover the even numbers and show the odd numbers.

EXTENSION WORK
◆ Ask the children to find out which numbers of cubes can be put into twos without having one left over. This establishes another aspect of even numbers: they can be 'paired' as well as being put into two equal groups. For example, 14 cubes make two equal towers (2 groups of 7) or seven pairs (7 groups of 2).
◆ Repeat the above activity to establish the concept of **odd numbers**.
◆ Ask the children what numbers they think can be put into two equal towers; use the language of 'sharing between'.

DOUBLE YOUR CUBES

GROUP SIZE AND ORGANIZATION
Whole-class demonstration, then pairs.
DURATION
30 minutes.
LEARNING OBJECTIVE
To develop an understanding of what doubling involves.

YOU WILL NEED
The colour poster, some 1–6 dice, interlocking cubes, photocopiable page 12, pencils.

WHAT TO DO
Tell the class that they are going to play a game using dice and cubes. Pick up a 1–6 dice; ask someone to roll it for you and call out the number. Ask the children to watch you carefully. Without explaining, make a stick with the 'called out' number of interlocking cubes. Now, still without explanation, make another identical stick and show both sticks to the children. Ask them to talk in their pairs and describe to each other what you have done. Ask several different children to describe it to the rest of the class. Pick up or develop the idea of **doubling**. Repeat the activity with more rolls of the dice.

Now give each pair a 1–6 dice, some interlocking cubes and a copy of photocopiable page 12. Ask them to do the same activity in pairs, recording the dice number and the 'double cubes' number on the sheet. They can take turns: child 1 rolls the dice, child 2 makes the first stick, then child 1 makes the second stick. They both work out the total number of cubes; if they agree, the number can be recorded on the sheet.

Encourage the children to say the doubles out loud, for example: 'Double 4 is 8'. Let them play for 10 to 15 minutes.

Now look at the colour poster together. Point to one of the dot patterns for 2s; ask the children which double is being shown, and how many dots there are. Repeat this process for several patterns. At this stage, it is enough for doubles to be recognized and talked about; there is no need to look at the formal recording of multiplication.

ASSESSMENT
Show the children two identical sticks of cubes. Can they recognize the double being shown, even if they can't tell you straight away how many cubes there are in total?

WORKING WITH 2S

Figure 2

IDEAS FOR DIFFERENTIATION
As a more challenging activity, children could use 0–9 dice or 0–10 digit cards to generate the numbers. Also, you could write some larger numbers in the 'Dice number' column on the photocopiable sheet for children to work with. Some children might like to put in their own larger numbers.

As a supporting activity, you could make a set of doubles using cubes (as in Figure 2) and then ask children to copy the set. Discuss with them the doubles they have made. To simplify the main activity, you could limit the numbers being doubled to the range 1–4 or 1–5. Other numbers on the dice could be covered up as blanks (meaning 'miss a go'), or replaced with smaller numbers.

DICE DOUBLES

GROUP SIZE AND ORGANIZATION
Whole-class demonstration, then pairs.
DURATION
40 minutes.
LEARNING OBJECTIVE
To learn the doubles of the numbers 1–6.

YOU WILL NEED
Photocopiable page 13, an A3 enlargement of the first pair of grids on page 13, pins or Blu-Tack, 1–6 and 0–9 dice, felt-tipped pens or crayons, a flip chart and marker pen (or chalkboard and chalk).

WHAT TO DO
Tell the children that they are going to play a doubling game. Ask them what 'doubling' means. Discuss with them how a double can be calculated:
◆ *Can it be worked out using a number line? How?* (For example, find 3 on the number line and then move on another 3.)
◆ *What other ways are there?* (Give the children a couple of examples to work out, such as double 4 and double 6. Some children may need to use cubes, but encourage them to find other ways of working out doubles. Some children may 'just know' some doubles.)

Although 0 does not feature in the main activity below, discuss the fact that double 0 is still 0. Use the number line to reinforce this point: taking no steps twice still gets you nowhere!

Ask two children to come out to the front. Pin up an enlarged copy of the top half of page 13, or draw the same grid twice on the flip chart. The players use a grid each:
1. Player 1 rolls the dice, calls out the number and works out its double.
2. If player 2 agrees, then player 1 colours in any square on his or her grid which shows that double number (for example, if 4 was rolled, 8 can be coloured in).
3. Player 2 then has a turn. Play continues with the players taking turns and colouring in squares on their own grids. If a player has a double which isn't one of the numbers left to be coloured in, he or she has to 'pass'.
4. The aim is to be the first player to colour in a complete line of seven squares. The line can be horizontal, vertical or diagonal.

2, 5 AND 10 TIMES TABLES

WORKING WITH 2S

Once the rules are understood, the children can play in pairs. After the initial demonstration, the game could be restricted to a 10-minute oral or mental activity. The children should play the game several times in order to develop instant recall of the doubles.

ASSESSMENT
When they play the game, note whether the children are 'working out' the doubles or instantly recalling them.

IDEAS FOR DIFFERENTIATION
Some children could go on to see which player fills in two lines or three lines, or completes the whole grid. A more challenging version of the game could be played with the 0–9 grids on photocopiable page 13.

EXTENSION WORK
The grids can be copied and adapted to contain larger numbers. Some commercially available dice show larger numbers. Alternatively, suitable numbers could be written onto blank dice or cubes.

TABLE TIME

GROUP SIZE AND ORGANIZATION
Whole class.
DURATION
20 minutes.
LEARNING OBJECTIVE
To build up the 2× table.

YOU WILL NEED
The colour poster, a piece of card (big enough to cover the 2× table on the poster), a flip chart and marker pen (or chalkboard and chalk).

WHAT TO DO
Display the poster and say that you are going to look together at the dot patterns arranged in 2s. *Can you see where they are?*

Encourage the children to describe each pattern as you point to it, and tell you how many dots there are. Link each pattern to the multiplication table on the poster, reading out each line. Discuss the use of the × symbol. Use the phrasing: '1 times 2 is 2, 2 times 2 is 4...' Ask the children to look at the last part of each multiplication (the 'answer'): 2, 4, 6... *What do you notice? Why is this happening? Why isn't 7 in this list?* Link this to previous work on counting in 2s, even numbers and doubling.

Now ask the children to close their eyes. Cover up one line of the multiplication table with your card. Ask them to open their eyes. Can they tell you which line you have covered up? Can they tell you what is written there? Can anyone write it on the flip chart? *Is that right? How do you know?*

Cover up one or more of the 'answers' and ask similar questions. Then ask: *Can anyone say what the next line would be if the table carried on?*

ASSESSMENT
Can the children read out the 2× table? Can they explain what it shows?

IDEAS FOR DISPLAY
Display the colour poster (or another version of the 2× table) with various elements covered up. Vary which features are hidden: sometimes numbers, sometimes the × or = sign. Put up a sign with the question: *What has been hidden?* This could be discussed each week.

WORKING WITH 2S

SHOW ME

GROUP SIZE AND ORGANIZATION
Whole class, then pairs.
DURATION
40 minutes.
LEARNING OBJECTIVE
To develop an understanding of multiplication represented as arrays of dots.

YOU WILL NEED
A 2 × 10 dot arrangement which all the children can see; all ten multiplications for the 2s written on separate pieces of card, large enough for the children to see (you could have a 0 × 2 card too); a piece of card to cover up some or all of the dot arrangement; Blu-Tack (optional); the colour poster; a flip chart and marker pen (or chalkboard and chalk); photocopiable page 14, scissors.

WHAT TO DO
Display a 2 × 10 dot array on the flip chart: either two rows of ten columns, or vice versa. (It might be interesting to repeat the activity another time, using the alternative orientation.) With all the class watching, show one of the multiplication cards. *Can we read this together?* Ask for a volunteer to come out and show this multiplication on the dot array, using a piece of card to cover the other dots (as in Figure 3). You could demonstrate one to start with – but ask the children what they think you are doing, rather than just telling them.

Continue to show different cards and identify the different dot patterns associated with each. In each case, ask how many dots can be seen and link this to the answer to the multiplication. If the cards are attached to the board with Blu-Tack, then after you have used them all, you could ask the children to put them in order.

Now look at the colour poster and ask the children to find the times table you have been working on. *What do you notice? Are there any multiplications missing? How do you know?* Encourage the whole class to say the table together, or invite individuals to try it.

Now ask the children to work in pairs. Give each pair a copy of photocopiable page 14. You or the children can cut along the dotted lines to separate the set of multiplications, the set of answers and the 2 × 10 dot array. Let the pairs play the 'Show me' game as follows:
1. The multiplication cards are shuffled and placed face down in a pile. The 'answer cards' are shuffled and dealt out to the two players, then spread out face up.
2. Player 1 turns over the top multiplication card, then uses his or her hand to cover part of the dot array so that the pattern matches the multiplication.
3. Both players check to see whether they have the appropriate answer card. Whoever has the card turns it over.
4. Player 2 now has a turn. The winner is the first player to turn over all his or her answer cards.

ASSESSMENT
Can the children identify the correct dot arrangement for a given multiplication?

MATCH IT

GROUP SIZE AND ORGANIZATION
Whole class, then pairs.
LEARNING OBJECTIVE
To become familiar with the 2 times table.
DURATION
30 minutes.

YOU WILL NEED
The colour poster; a large piece of paper to cover the times tables section; photocopiable page 14 (only the number and multiplication cards from page 14 are needed; they could be photocopied onto thin card for repeated use).

WHAT TO DO
Look at the colour poster together and ask a child to identify the 2 times table: the multiplication table for 2s. Read it with the children, pointing to each line as you all say it.

Figure 3

2, 5 AND 10 TIMES TABLES — RESOURCE BANK

WORKING WITH 2S

Now cover up the multiplication table. Ask whether anyone knows any of the multiplications in the 2× table. Discuss the ones the children know, and how they can work out those they cannot remember. If no-one has suggested it, use fingers to count out: show 4 × 2 as 2, 4, 6, 8 (with four fingers shown). Relate the 2× table to earlier work on doubles. Encourage the children to explain how they can find the answers. Now uncover the poster and look again at the 2× table.

The children can go on to do a matching activity. Give each pair a set of 'multiplication' cards and a set of 'answer' cards (photocopied from page 14). These cards can be used in several ways:

◆ The children can simply sort the cards to find the matching pairs, put them in order and read them out to each other.

◆ The 'answer' cards can be dealt out and the 'multiplication' cards left on the table face down in a pile. One at a time, the multiplication cards are turned over; whoever has the matching answer card places it on top of the multiplication card. The first person to run out of answer cards is the winner. (Alternatively, the answer cards can be left face down in a pile and the multiplication cards dealt out.)

◆ For more players, two (or more) sets could be used in the same way. The first player to call out the correct response can place his or her card.

ASSESSMENT
Can the children order the multiplication facts in the 2× table correctly? Are they beginning to know some of these facts?

DINOSAUR GAME

GROUP SIZE AND ORGANIZATION
Whole class, then pairs.
DURATION
40 minutes.
LEARNING OBJECTIVE
To practise the recall of facts in the 2 times table.

YOU WILL NEED
Photocopiable page 15, some 0–9 dice, counters, the colour poster, a piece of card (to cover lines in the times table). **NB** Commercial ten-sided dice are available from some school suppliers such as NES Arnold, and from 'war game' suppliers such as Games Workshop.

WHAT TO DO
Ask the children to look at the 2 times table on the colour poster. Ask someone to come and show the class which one it is. Encourage the children to read it out, perhaps as a whole class. Ask one of the children to come and point to each part of the table as it is read out.

As before, cover up a line or some lines of the multiplication table and ask the children what is hidden. Now try covering up the column of 'answers' and asking the children, in pairs, to decide on the answers to random multiplications that you choose. Then try giving an answer and asking which multiplication it belongs to.

The children can now play the 'dinosaur game':
1. Player 1 rolls the dice and multiplies the number by 2.
2. If player 2 agrees with the answer, and the answer is on player 1's dinosaur, then player 1 can cover it up with a counter.
3. Player 2 now has a turn. The players continue to alternate.
4. Decide on a rule for the winner. It could be the first player to cover up eight numbers, or the first to cover up all his or her numbers.

ASSESSMENT
Can the children give the correct answers when multiplying different numbers by 2?

WORKING WITH 2S

Name —————————— Date ——————————

Join the dots

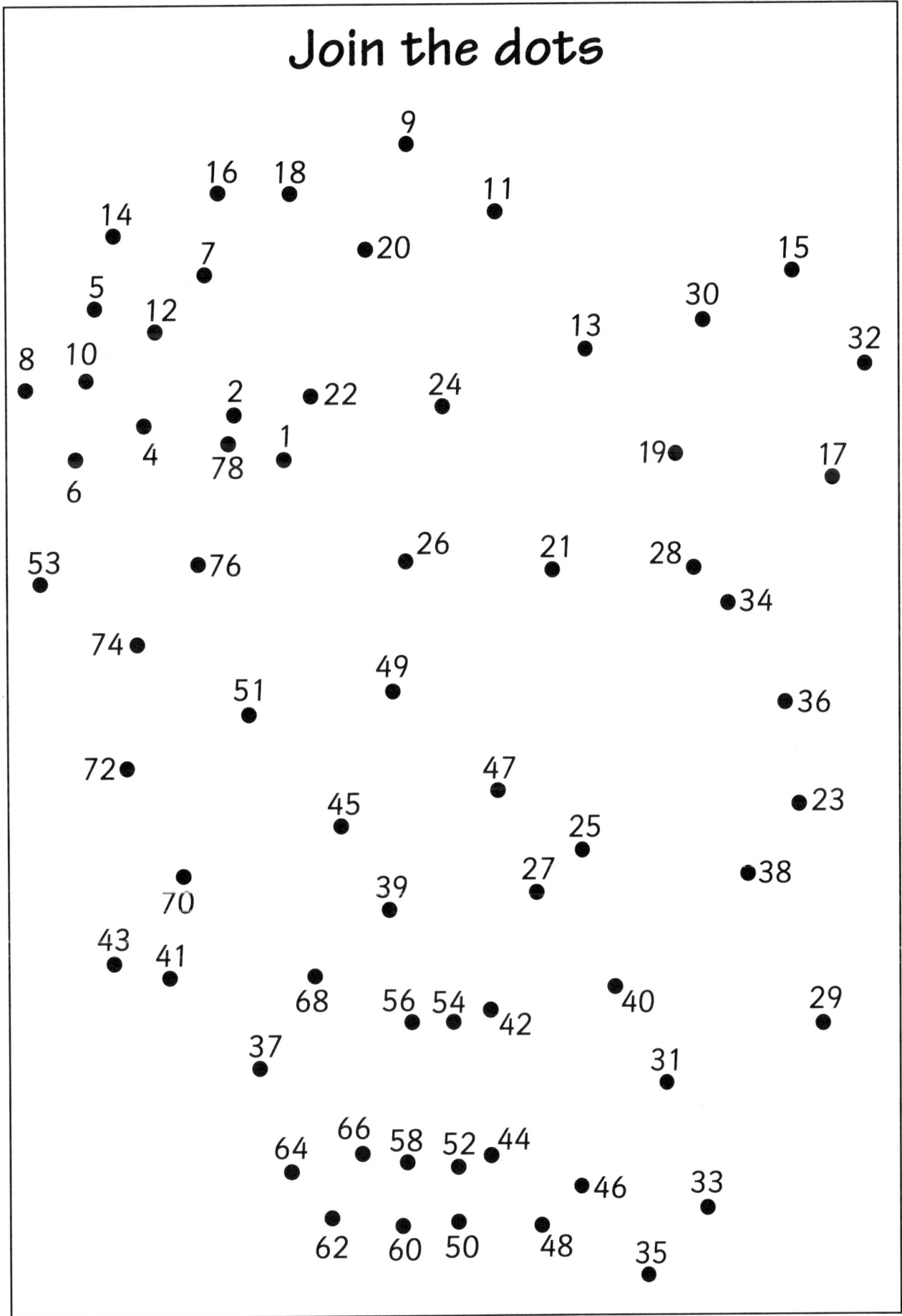

2, 5 AND 10 TIMES TABLES

WORKING WITH 2S

Name —————————————— Date ——————————

Double your cubes

Dice number	Double cubes	Dice number	Double cubes
◯ ·····> ◯		◯ ·····> ◯	
◯ ·····> ◯		◯ ·····> ◯	
◯ ·····> ◯		◯ ·····> ◯	
◯ ·····> ◯		◯ ·····> ◯	
◯ ·····> ◯		◯ ·····> ◯	

WORKING WITH 2S

Name _____   Date _____

Dice doubles

These grids are for use with 1–6 dice:

10	4	10	6	8	2	6
2	6	12	10	2	6	10
6	8	4	2	8	12	8
4	8	12	4	10	12	2
8	2	4	10	8	6	10
4	6	10	12	2	12	2
2	12	4	8	12	6	4

10	4	10	6	8	2	6
2	6	12	10	2	6	10
6	8	4	2	8	12	8
4	8	12	4	10	12	2
8	2	4	10	8	6	10
4	6	10	12	2	12	2
2	12	4	8	12	6	4

These grids are for use with 0–9 dice:

0	4	2	16	6	10	16
16	0	18	14	2	0	18
10	8	10	2	6	4	0
12	12	4	14	12	18	4
14	0	2	6	8	12	18
18	4	8	10	16	6	10
16	12	6	14	10	14	8

0	4	2	16	6	10	16
16	0	18	14	2	0	18
10	8	10	2	6	4	0
12	12	4	14	12	18	4
14	0	2	6	8	12	18
18	4	8	10	16	6	10
16	12	6	14	10	14	8

WORKING WITH 2S

Name _____   Date _____

Show me				
2	4	6	8	10
12	14	16	18	20
6 × 2	7 × 2	8 × 2	9 × 2	10 × 2
1 × 2	2 × 2	3 × 2	4 × 2	5 × 2

● ● ● ● ● ● ● ● ● ●
● ● ● ● ● ● ● ● ● ●

WORKING WITH 2S

Name _____ Date _____

Dinosaur game

WORKING WITH 5S

GIVE ME FIVE!

GROUP SIZE AND ORGANIZATION
Whole class sitting in a circle.
DURATION
10–15 minutes.
LEARNING OBJECTIVE
To practise counting in 5s with a visual link.

YOU WILL NEED
50 Multilink cubes in sticks of five. For extension: a class number line, the black and white poster, photocopiable page 20.

WHAT TO DO
Choose ten children sitting together and give each child a stick of five Multilink cubes. Establish they have five cubes each. Explain that you are going to point to each child in turn; as you do so, the child should hold up (and keep up) his or her five cubes. The rest of the class should count on in 5s as the cubes are raised. You may wish to demonstrate this. Encourage everyone to join in, counting in 5s up to 50. Repeat if necessary to reinforce the pattern.

Cubes down! Now ask the first three children to hold up their cubes. *How many cubes are held up? Check with the person sitting next to you. How did you know?* Acknowledge all responses, but reinforce those which used counting in 5s. Repeat this with other numbers of children.

ASSESSMENT
This activity can be repeated many times, with or without the cubes. Not all the children will know the full sequence of numbers initially, but gradually they will become familiar with them.

EXTENSION WORK
The children could go on to find the 5s numbers on the class number line. They could also look at the black and white poster and identify the 5s numbers on the 1–25 grid. *Where are the numbers? Why? If the grid had more rows, but was still in 5s, where would 30 be? Why? What about 35?*

Photocopiable page 20 could be used as a follow-up. The children should join the dots on the picture and see a cat's face.

BUILD IT UP

GROUP SIZE AND ORGANIZATION
Whole class.
DURATION
20 minutes.
LEARNING OBJECTIVE
To build up the 5 times table using rows of dots.

YOU WILL NEED
The colour poster, a piece of paper (to cover the whole 5 times table), a card (to cover one line of the table at a time), cards of 5× facts and Blu-Tack (optional), a board or flip chart, a pegboard and pegs.

WHAT TO DO
For this activity, cover up the 5 times table in such a way that a line at a time can be uncovered.

With all the children watching, put a row (or column) of five pegs on your pegboard. Ask the children what you have done. Value all contributions, but come back to any comments about a row or set of 5. Uncover the first line of the table on the poster, with its dot pattern.

Now put in another row of pegs. Ask the children what you have done and what they can see now. Follow through any comments about two sets or rows of five pegs. Uncover the second row of the table on the poster. Continue like this; when you feel it is appropriate, ask the children what they think you will do next. Encourage them to predict the next line and to suggest what it will 'say' (the relevant multiplication fact).

When you have completed the pattern up to ten rows of five, ask the children to think about this pattern. What do they notice about it? Asking them, in pairs, to think of four things they notice can be a good

WORKING WITH 5S

way of getting them to talk about the multiplication patterns. After a few minutes, 'collect' their observations. Ask them to explain what they have noticed. Some of their comments should relate to number endings (0 and 5); if not, ask how the numbers end. Reinforce this by saying the 5× table together, with you starting off.

Now cover up a line of the table and ask the children what is missing. Ask the other children whether they think the answer is right, and how they know. Try covering up two lines, or covering up different parts of a line.

You could also use a set of cards, each showing a different line of the table. Shuffle them, then stick them on the board in random order. See how quickly a child can put them in the right order.

ASSESSMENT
Can the children associate a dot pattern with the 5× table? Can they predict the next line in the table? Can they see a pattern in the numbers?

IDEAS FOR DISPLAY
Display the colour poster on the wall. Using small paper clouds or stars, cover up different parts of the 5× table: some numbers and some non-number symbols. Put up the question: *Can you work out what is covered up?* At the end of the week, spend a few minutes discussing this question with the children; then move the clouds (or ask a child to move them) to new places.

1. The number cards are shuffled and dealt out to the two players, who spread them out face up. The multiplication cards are shuffled and placed, face down, in a pile. The dot pattern is placed so that both players can reach it easily.
2. Player 1 turns over the top multiplication card from the pile. Using a hand or a piece of paper, player 1 'shows' the correct dot pattern to represent this multiplication (as in Figure 4).
3. The player who has the number card with the answer to this multiplication says the number. If the other player agrees, the 'answer' card is turned over. Player 2 then has a turn.
4. The first player to turn over all his or her cards is the winner. Play the game several times.

ASSESSMENT
Can the children identify the correct dot arrangement for a given multiplication?

Figure 4

TOTALLY DOTTY

GROUP SIZE AND ORGANIZATION
Whole-class demonstration; game in pairs.
DURATION
15 minutes for game.
LEARNING OBJECTIVE
To develop an understanding of how multiplication can be represented spatially.

YOU WILL NEED
Photocopiable page 21 (one copy per pair, cut into cards and dot grid; an A3 copy of the sheet, similarly cut up).

WHAT TO DO
Ask for two volunteers to demonstrate the game to the whole class (using the enlarged cards and grid):

COLLECT YOUR MONEY

GROUP SIZE AND ORGANIZATION
Pairs.
DURATION
20 minutes.
LEARNING OBJECTIVE
To practise counting in 5s using 5p coins.

YOU WILL NEED
A flipchart and marker pen (or chalkboard and chalk), a class number line or grid, 5p coins, 0–9 dice, photocopiable page 22.

WHAT TO DO
Photocopiable page 22 can also be used to give the children practice in counting in 2s or 10s (see 'Ideas for differentiation').

2, 5 AND 10 TIMES TABLES

WORKING WITH 5S

Give each pair nine 5p pieces, a 0–9 dice and a strip of money boxes photocopied from page 22. Draw large versions of the money boxes on the flip chart, and use these to demonstrate the game to the class: Player 1 rolls the dice and collects that number of 5p coins. He or she counts out the total amount in 5s and states it to his or her partner. If the partner agrees, player 1 puts a tick underneath his or her money box showing that amount. Player 2 then has a turn.

Decide how the winner will be determined. It could be the first player to have a tick underneath every box, to have two ticks underneath every box, to have a tick underneath six boxes in a row, and so on. Change the rules for winning on subsequent occasions.

Counting out loud (but not too loud!) and agreeing or disagreeing are important aspects of this game. Make it clear to the children that you will be looking and listening to check that they are playing properly. If a player rolls 0, he or she collects no money.

Bring the children together at the end to practise counting in 5s. Ask a child to point to each number on a number line or grid as it is spoken.

ASSESSMENT
Can the children count in 5s using 5p coins? Can they recognize the written amounts of money?

IDEAS FOR DIFFERENTIATION
This activity could also be used with 2p coins to practise counting in 2s, or with 10p coins to practise counting in 10s. Photocopiable page 22 contains three strips, one for use with each coin.

IDEAS FOR DISPLAY
An enlarged strip from page 22 could be put up with a question such as: *How many 5p coins will be needed for these money boxes?* Go beyond 45p if appropriate.

EXTENSION WORK
Write the different money box amounts on large cards. Mix them up, then show a card to the class. Can they work out how many 5p coins are needed to make this amount? They could check with their partners: do they agree? Collect responses. Continue with the rest of the cards, repeating if appropriate.

RACE TRACKS

GROUP SIZE AND ORGANIZATION
Whole class, then pairs.
DURATION
30 minutes.
LEARNING OBJECTIVE
To practise multiplying by 5.

YOU WILL NEED
The colour poster, pieces of paper and Blu-Tack (to cover the answers), a flip chart and marker pen (or chalkboard and chalk), 0–9 dice, photocopiable page 23, coloured pens.

WHAT TO DO
Put up the colour poster and explain that you are going to look at the 5 times table. Ask different children to say different lines; then, perhaps, ask all of the children to say the table together.

Cover up the answers and go down the table, asking for the missing numbers. Now ask for the missing numbers at random. Discuss with children how they remember the answers, or how they work them out. Some of their strategies may include: counting in 5s; using fingers to show sets of 5; halving answers from known 10× facts; working backwards from (or forwards to) other 5× facts. You may need to work with the children on some of these strategies, perhaps over a period of time.

Demonstrate the Race Track game to the class. You may want to draw a large version of a grid on the board before you start. Each child will need a grid photocopied from page 23 and a coloured pen. The first grid is simpler because the multiples of 5 are in order; you can decide which children need to use this one first.

Ask the children to look at the 'column' numbers along the bottom of the grid. These are the 'race track numbers'. As the game progresses, they will colour in one square at a time up the tracks.

Player 1 rolls the dice, multiplies that number by 5 and gives the answer to his or her partner. If the partner agrees, player 1 colours in one square of that number's race track on her or his own grid. The squares should be coloured in one at a time, starting from the bottom of the track (as in Figure 5). Player 2 then has a turn.

The winner is the first player to fill in any one of the race tracks to the end. The players could play on for a second winning track, a third and so on.

WORKING WITH 5S

Figure 5

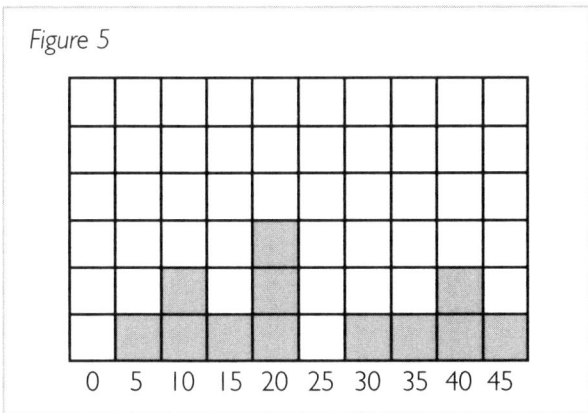

ASSESSMENT
Do the children know any of the multiplication facts in the 5× table? Do they have any strategies for working out facts that they don't know?

IDEAS FOR DIFFERENTIATION
This game could also be used to practise multiplying by 2 or by 10: the new 'column' numbers could be written on the photocopiable grid.

GRIDLOCK

GROUP SIZE AND ORGANIZATION
Whole class, then groups or pairs.
DURATION
30–45 minutes, or several sessions of 10–15 minutes.
LEARNING OBJECTIVE
To identify patterns within a number grid.

YOU WILL NEED
The black and white poster, photocopies (several per child) of the 1–25 grid from the poster, coloured pens, scissors, squared paper, Post-It notes.

WHAT TO DO
Look at the black and white poster with the children. Talk about the 1–25 grid. *What is the smallest number? Which number is greatest? How many numbers are there altogether? How many in each row? In each column?*

Ask the children to name any number on the grid. *Add on 5. What number do you get? Add on 10. What number do you get now?*

Cover some of the numbers with 'Post-It' notes. *Which numbers are hidden? How do you know?*

Let the children work (in pairs or groups) on photocopies of the 1–25 grid, using coloured pens.

They could:
◆ colour in all the multiples of 5;
◆ put the correct number of dots in each square that shows a multiple of 5 (relating counting skills to actual numbers);
◆ make a jigsaw by cutting up the grid, then rearrange the numbers in a variety of patterns;
◆ colour all the multiples of 10 in yellow, then all the other multiples of 5 in red;
◆ add another row of numbers, continuing the pattern;
◆ copy out a blank grid, then write in the multiples of 5.

ASSESSMENT
Encourage the children to use precise language when they explain their thinking (for example, challenge any ambiguous statement). A response to the question *Which numbers are in the 5 times table?* provides important assessment data: the answer *5, 10, 15...* is correct, but the answer *Any number ending in a 5 or 0* is more complete and shows a higher level of understanding.

IDEAS FOR DIFFERENTIATION
Most of these ideas could be adapted for other grids and numerical arrangements.

IDEAS FOR DISPLAY
Make a large version of the 1–25 grid with individual number squares; move some of the squares around at various times. In your mental maths sessions, make it a routine question to ask the children which numbers are in the wrong place. *How do you know they are in the wrong place?* Turn some numbers to face the wall, and ask the children to say which numbers are 'hiding'. Add another blank row to the grid and ask the children to write in the correct numbers.

2, 5 AND 10 TIMES TABLES — RESOURCE BANK

WORKING WITH 5S

Name _____ Date _____

Dot to dot

◆ Fill in the missing numbers:

5, —, 15, 20, —, 30, 35, —, —, 50, 55, 60, —, —, —, 80, —.

◆ Join up the same numbers to make a picture.
You will not need to use all the dots.

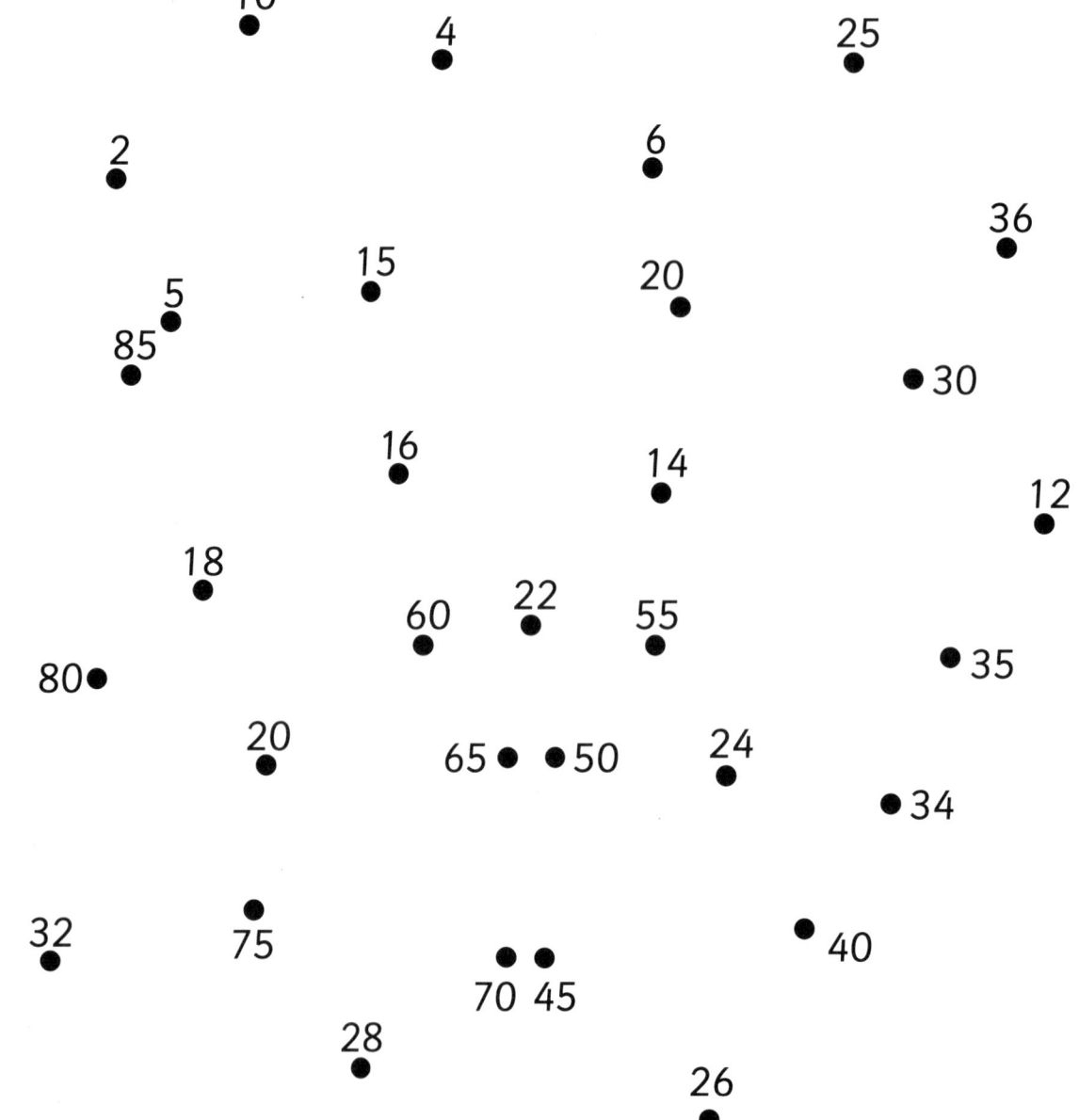

◆ When you have finished, draw in some eyes.

WORKING WITH 5S

Cards and dot grid

5	10	15	20	25
30	35	40	45	50
2 × 5	4 × 5	6 × 5	8 × 5	10 × 5
1 × 5	3 × 5	5 × 5	7 × 5	9 × 5

WORKING WITH 5S

Money boxes

Row 1: 2p, 4p, 6p, 8p, 10p, 12p, 14p, 16p, 18p

Row 2: 5p, 10p, 15p, 20p, 25p, 30p, 35p, 40p, 45p

Row 3: 10p, 20p, 30p, 40p, 50p, 60p, 70p, 80p, 90p

WORKING WITH 5S

Name —————————————— Date ——————————————

Race tracks

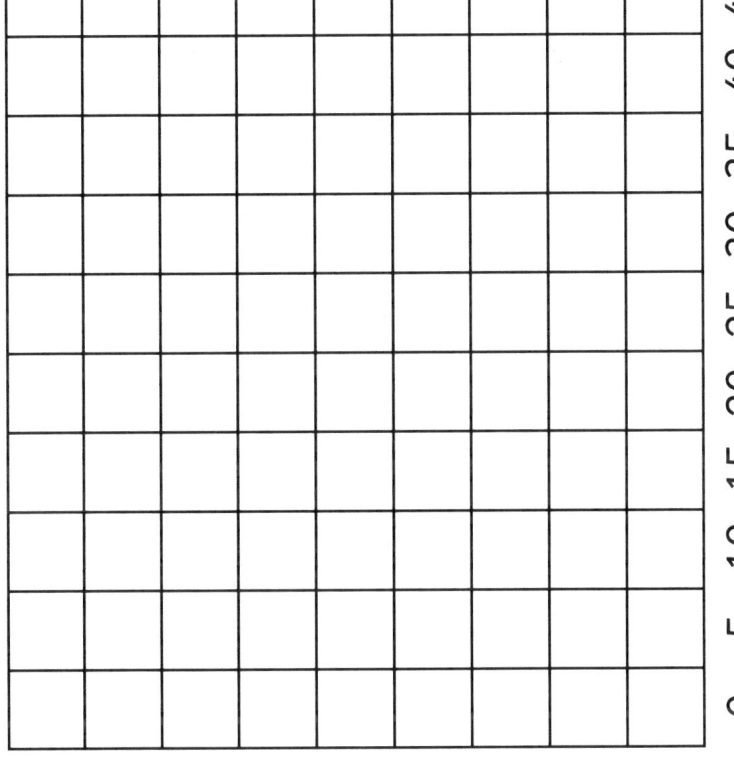
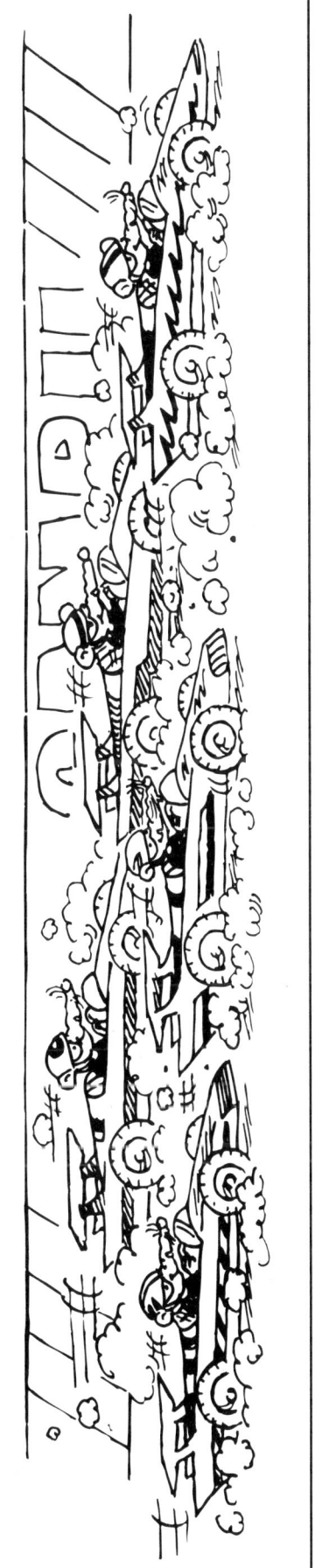

2, 5 AND 10 TIMES TABLES

PHOTOCOPIABLE RESOURCE BANK

23

WORKING WITH 10S

STAR SPOTS

GROUP SIZE AND ORGANIZATION
Whole class, then pairs or individuals.
DURATION
30–45 minutes.
LEARNING OBJECTIVE
To recognize multiples of 10 up to 100.

YOU WILL NEED
The black and white poster, Blu-Tack, small fluorescent stars (available from office suppliers) or pieces of paper, photocopiable page 27, pens, a calculator or other display of digital numbers (for example, on a digital clock).

WHAT TO DO
Display the black and white poster. Talk about the number patterns shown in the 10 times table. Encourage the children to say the '10, 20...' pattern out loud. Read the 10× table aloud. Ask the children to continue with the number pattern of 10s, if you feel this is appropriate. Ask questions such as: *What number comes after 100? And after 120?* Ask the children to repeat the 10× table forwards and backwards. *What number would come next? Can you continue the table beyond 100?*

Use fluorescent stars and Blu-Tack to hide some of the numbers. For example, you could hide 50 and ask: *Which number is hidden? Is it larger than 60? Is it between 30 and 40? Is it even? Can you write it?* If so, ask the children to write it down. Check the numeral they have written.

Can you find it on a calculator? Compare the printed numeral and the digital version. *Can you describe the different forms of this numeral? Can you find examples of it around the room?*

Reveal the number. Now reverse the game by asking children to come out and hide a number that:
◆ is greater than 60 but less than 80;
◆ or has a 0 and a 9 in it;
◆ or is between 30 and 70; and so on.

Now play the Star Spots game. Give each child or pair a copy of photocopiable page 27. Ask the children to say which numbers are hidden, and to write the correct number above each star. They should then write all the 'hidden' numbers **that are in the 10 times table** in the box at the bottom of the sheet. At the end, gather all the children together and collect their 'box' numbers. Check whether they know all of the 10s numbers up to 100. Comment on the similarity of these numbers: they all end with a 0.

IDEAS FOR DISPLAY
Make a large display version of a 100 square; use coloured paper stars to hide some of the numbers. Provide stars with (handwritten) 'digital' numbers on, and ask the children to put the correct 'star numbers' in the correct spaces. Use the display to show that digital numbers are the same as 'normal' numbers: they just have a slightly different appearance.

PEGGY PATTERNS

GROUP SIZE AND ORGANIZATION
Whole class, then pairs.
DURATION
35–45 minutes.
LEARNING OBJECTIVES
To explore number bonds of 10. To practise counting in multiples of 10 up to 100.

YOU WILL NEED
The black and white poster, 10 × 10 pegboards, coloured pegs, photocopiable page 28, 1–6 dice, coloured pens or pencils.

WHAT TO DO
Introduce the activity by asking the children to say the pattern of 10s.

WORKING WITH 10S

Display a pegboard. Ask a child to put ten pegs in a row and then add another ten to make 20. As the pegs are placed, the other children can count aloud. Now show the children the faces of a 1–6 dice and ask them to say what the numbers are.

Select an empty pegboard (10 × 10) and ask a child to roll a pair of dice. Explain that the aim is to complete rows of 10. For example, if the dice show a 3 and 5, the child can **either** put 3 pegs in one row and 5 in another **or** make a row of 8. For the next throw, the child might roll a 2 and a 4. He or she can start a new row, start two new rows or complete rows already started (in this case, making a row of 10 by adding the 2 on to the 8).

Let the children play the game in pairs. Give each pair a pegboard and pegs, two 1–6 dice, two coloured pens and two copies of photocopiable page 28. For each row completed on the pegboard, a child can colour in one stepping stone on his or her game sheet. The winner is the first child to colour in enough stones to cross the river.

ASSESSMENT
Ask the children how they could make 10, and how they could make 20. Also ask them to say how many pegs make 2 full rows, 3 full rows, and so on up to 10 full rows.

IDEAS FOR DISPLAY
A large stepping-stone display of 10s could be incorporated into another display, such as a river picture.

EXTENSION WORK
The game could be played using different kinds of dice, or steps other than 10.

EYES CLOSED

GROUP SIZE AND ORGANIZATION
Whole class, then pairs or individuals.
DURATION
35–45 minutes.
LEARNING OBJECTIVES
To recognize patterns of numbers in the 2, 5 and 10 times tables. To check the 'reasonableness' of answers.

YOU WILL NEED
The black and white poster, a flip chart and marker pen (or chalkboard and chalk), photocopiable page 29 (see 'Ideas for differentiation'), pens in three different colours, a list of numbers (see 'What to do').

WHAT TO DO
Look together at the black and white poster. Ask the children to tell you four things they notice about each of the number grids (in turn). Record their observations – including any inaccurate ones! Ask the children which ideas they agree and disagree with.

Now ask the children to close their eyes and describe the grids. Ask some introductory questions about the 1–16 grid to focus their attention on the number arrangement – for example: *Which number is next to 5? Which number is just above 12? What is the first number? What is the largest odd number?*

Repeat this with the 1–25 grid, but include questions about multiples – for example: *Which numbers are in the 2 times table? What about the 5 times table? The 10 times table? Are any of the numbers in more than one times table? Which ones?* Allow the children to reassure themselves of their answers when they re-open their eyes.

WORKING WITH 10S

Write a multiple of 5 on the flip chart that is not on the grid (such as 55). Ask the children whether they think it is in the 5 times table. Ask them to explain how they know whether it is in the 5 times table. Repeat with some other multiples of 5; then some multiples of 10; then some multiples of 2. Ask the children to explain how they recognize multiples of 2, 5 or 10.

Give the children a list of numbers and ask them whether each number is a multiple of 2, 5 or 10. Ask about common multiples – for example: *Is 80 only in the 10 times table, or is it in any other? How do you know?*

IDEAS FOR DIFFERENTIATION
Give each child a copy of photocopiable page 29. Ask the children to colour in numbers that are in the 2, 5 and 10 times tables (in different colours). Children could use the same sheet for all three tables or use a separate sheet for each table, according to their ability. If the children work in pairs, ask them to tell each other how they have decided which numbers are the correct multiples. They cannot use the argument *Because they are!*

SAY IT OUT LOUD

GROUP SIZE AND ORGANIZATION
Whole class, then individuals or pairs.
DURATION
30 minutes.
LEARNING OBJECTIVE
To revise the 2, 5 and/or 10 times tables.

YOU WILL NEED
The colour poster; cards made from photocopiable pages 30, 31 and/or 32 (if possible, copy these onto card and laminate them); blank cards.

WHAT TO DO
This activity can be done with the 2, 5 and/or 10 times table, using the cards provided on the appropriate photocopiable page. The main idea is to get the children to say the number sentences out loud (which will take up most of the session); the cards are a means of encouraging this. The lesson plan below refers to all three sets of times tables cards; substitute examples from your chosen times table(s) when you come to do the activity.

Introduce the cards. Check that the children can read and understand the words on them.

For each pair, choose 12 cards that make up three complete multiplication sentences. Jumble the cards, then ask the pair to arrange some of them to make one complete, accurate sentence. When they have done this, ask the children (one at a time) to read the cards out loud in the correct order. Can they go on to recite the complete times table?

Now give each child or pair a set of cards. Try the following activities:
◆ Ask the children to find out whether there are any numbers that have more than one card.
◆ Provide some blank cards and ask the children to write numbers to make an accurate number sentence of their own, using one of these cards with other cards in each sentence.
◆ Take out the word cards; then mix up the number cards and ask the children to place each set in order.
◆ In a plenary session, ask the children to describe the number patterns in the times tables. *Can you think of a symbol or a number to put in place of the word 'are' or the word 'twos'? Can you make a sentence that has symbols rather than words?*

IDEAS FOR DIFFERENTIATION
To make the activity more challenging for some children, ask them to:
◆ use blank cards to extend the table beyond ×10;
◆ use cards to make a sentence for '20 2s are…';
◆ mix two sets of cards together (for example, from the 2 and 5 times tables), then repeat all the activities above.

WORKING WITH 10S

Name _____   Date _____

Star numbers

1 2 3 4 5 6 7 8 9 ☆

11 12 ☆ 14 15 16 17 18 19 ☆

☆ 22 23 24 25 26 27 28 29 30

31 32 33 34 35 36 37 38 39 ☆

41 42 43 44 ☆ 46 47 48 49 50

51 52 53 54 55 56 57 58 59 ☆

61 62 ☆ 64 65 66 67 68 69 70

71 72 73 74 75 76 77 78 79 80

☆ 82 83 84 85 ☆ 87 88 89 90

91 92 93 94 95 96 97 98 99 ☆

◆ Write all the 'star numbers' that are 10s here.

2, 5 AND 10 TIMES TABLES

WORKING WITH 10S

Stepping stones

Each time you make a row of ten pegs, you can colour in a stepping stone. The winner is the one who crosses the river first.

WORKING WITH 10S

Name _____ Date _____

Dream numbers

The frog is dreaming of being a prince.
He is also dreaming of some numbers.

◆ Can you break the spell by colouring in any numbers that are in the _____ times table?

2	32	5	10
57	28	8	21
13	7	4	12
3	1	16	15
20	24	30	35
6	17	40	25
9	14	27	100

◆ Can you make up some dream numbers of your own?

2, 5 AND 10 TIMES TABLES

WORKING WITH 10S

2 times table cards

1	two	is	2
2	twos	are	4
3	twos	are	6
4	twos	are	8
5	twos	are	10
6	twos	are	12
7	twos	are	14
8	twos	are	16
9	twos	are	18
10	twos	are	20

PHOTOCOPIABLE RESOURCE BANK

WORKING WITH 10S

5 times table cards

1	five	is	5
2	fives	are	10
3	fives	are	15
4	fives	are	20
5	fives	are	25
6	fives	are	30
7	fives	are	35
8	fives	are	40
9	fives	are	45
10	fives	are	50

WORKING WITH 10S

10 times table cards

1	ten	is	10
2	tens	are	20
3	tens	are	30
4	tens	are	40
5	tens	are	50
6	tens	are	60
7	tens	are	70
8	tens	are	80
9	tens	are	90
10	tens	are	100